The Water Hose

An Autobiographical Sketch
of Struggle and Hope

Tristan James

BALBOA.
PRESS

A DIVISION OF HAY HOUSE

Balboa Press books may be ordered through booksellers or by contacting:

Balboa Press
A Division of Hay House
1663 Liberty Drive
Bloomington, IN 47403
www.balboapress.com
1 (877) 407-4847

Because of the dynamic nature of the Internet, any web addresses or links contained in this book may have changed since publication and may no longer be valid. The views expressed in this work are solely those of the author and do not necessarily reflect the views of the publisher, and the publisher hereby disclaims any responsibility for them.

The author of this book does not dispense medical advice or prescribe the use of any technique as a form of treatment for physical, emotional, or medical problems without the advice of a physician, either directly or indirectly. The intent of the author is only to offer information of a general nature to help you in your quest for emotional and spiritual well-being. In the event you use any of the information in this book for yourself, which is your constitutional right, the author and the publisher assume no responsibility for your actions.

Any people depicted in stock imagery provided by Thinkstock are models, and such images are being used for illustrative purposes only.
Certain stock imagery © Thinkstock.

Print information available on the last page.

ISBN: 978-1-5043-3136-4 (sc)
ISBN: 978-1-5043-3137-1 (e)

Library of Congress Control Number: 2015905700

Balboa Press rev. date: 05/03/2015

To Ailee, you gave me the courage
to pick up the pen again.

Praise For Tristan James' "The Water Hose…"

"Tristan…I see all the hard hitting things you've been doing in the community. Your punches are making a difference, trust me. Your uppercuts are knocking down things like poverty, homelessness and hunger. I'm so proud of you Tristan. You're the real champion! May God continue to bless you in your endeavours." - **MIKE TYSON, UNDISPUTED HEAVYWEIGHT CHAMPION OF THE WORLD**

"Tristan, I've heard a lot about you and the impact you are having on people's lives. It seems from the stories I hear you've grown so much from when you were 15 years old to the man you've become. You are a true inspiration to me." - **BRIAN BOITANO, OLYMPIC FIGURE SKATING GOLD MEDALIST**

"It's really great see all of the positivity and wholeness that you're passing along to everyone. It's one step closer to making the world a more peaceful place." - **KIM LIGHT, FRIEND**

"Every time I would ever give a speech in class I would literally just do my best impression of you. I was gone a long time from school from really bad depression and only two people ever tried to contact me when I was gone. I always regretted not messaging you back and just saying thank you…but just being able to partake in the Tristan James experience was a great thing." - **L.J., FRIEND**

Tristan's journey is one that everyone should know today. I knew his journey before reading this, but physically reading it leaves me speechless on how incredible his journey is and where he is today. - **KAYEN WILBORN, FRIEND**

Contents

Foreword

Life is not something you aren't familiar with. Holding this book in your hands, you breathe while your heartbeats; you are living. For the past twenty, forty, sixty years you've aspired to be everything you can be, dreamed to attain a certain goal, but along the way you were cut, bruised, broken by life itself. It wasn't your fault, but in your journey from birth to now, you've absorbed punches, rode over bumps in the road, fallen to the lowest points, however, you are still here, still able to accomplish the dreams you dreamt yesterday!

You didn't pick up this title by accident, nor did you go through the pain of the past without a purpose. Your pain has a purpose. Each heartbreak, each mistake, and setback was simply a setup for another chance to pick yourself up off the mat, to show your strength, and to show others that despite all that is chasing you, you can run a little bit faster.

It is my hope that "The Water Hose: An Autobiographical Sketch on Struggle and Hope" will be a tool for you to confront your fears, so that you can live the victorious life you've been destined for!

Tristan James.

An Open Letter

Since August 2014, I've been attending Virginia Commonwealth University in the heart of Richmond, Virginia. The city, and University is a place where I've been able to expand my dreams exponentially, because of the immense size of Richmond. However, reflecting on it's size and the people within the city limits I've thought often of Madison. The skyscrapers of Fortune 500 companies, malls, and shops of Richmond are all illustrious and well respected, yet even with all of Richmond's mammoth glitz and glamour I have found that it simply can not compare to the simplicity of the little county in the foothills of the Blue Ridge mountains.

Recently, I returned from an internship with Joel Osteen Ministries and being able to serve people with Pastor Joel Osteen I learned many things about God's plan for His children. With Joel I saw that God takes ordinary people and uses them to do extraordinary things. In the Bible, we see God use David, a small shepherd boy, to overcome Goliath. Similarly, He uses Mary, a simple handmaid, to bring about the greatest blessing the world has ever known. In Madison, I see God using the ordinary to bring about the extraordinary.

There's something about watching Mr. John Berry run around, capture and immortalize in his photographs the efforts of incredible student-athletes and crazy fans or when the stress of the week becomes too much to bear, nothing compares to finding relief in hearing the preaching of Rev. Jeff Light or Alan Follet. When your car breaks down, you know Mr. O.J. Weaver has already taken care of you before your car even enters his shop in Criglersville. There is simply an unseen beauty in going to the drugstore and getting a malt, D&K's barbershop to get a haircut, McDonalds to get a happy meal, Preddy's Funeral Home to pay your respects.

Madison will never be physically as big or as flashy as Richmond, but within Madison are people with big dreams and large hopes. These people are who I think about each day, the people I fight for everyday I am in Richmond. Madison, will always be the town that made me, the town that gave birth to my dreams, the town I buried my father in, the town that has become my heartbeat. Because even though Richmond is a huge blessing, the mountains reflect a certain beauty that the skyscrapers never could. Reflected in these old blue mountains are the thousands of cows in the field, the country church steeples, the high school that lines 29, the drugstore on Main St., the lodge with it's many apples in the hills of Syria, and the people whose only desire is to live a simple life filled with love. This is the county I get to call home, these are the people I get to call family.

Wherever I am called to go to change someone's life, I will never forget Madison.

Thank you for your continued support in all my dreams and aspirations.

Tristan James
April 22, 2015

Chapter 1

Everything Has Beginning

In the darkness of my bedroom red digits began to flash, the alarm clock sounded. I stumbled out of bed to begin getting ready for school. My desk lamp was on from the night before and the calendar read, April 22, 2011, "Good Friday". The idea that a god would have so much love for those who turned their back on him, by giving all of himself, always amazed me.

—✴—

Out of immense pressure comes life. Nothing can become anything without an agent of change, something which transforms how things are perceived into something completely different. The water hose is the greatest example of this. Rushing from it's mouth is the basis for which growth occurs, the foundation for change. We cannot enjoy the simple things of life without the help of a water hose. It's incredible that a 25ft piece of vinyl contributes to the whole of society in such tremendous ways that we don't even notice. A seed becomes a flower through the aid of the water hose. The shelter from the summer sun, a swimming pool, is filled by what is given from the water hose.

I was born Tristan Lee James on December 27, 1995, at St. Mary's Hospital in Richmond, Virginia to Randy Lee James and Michelle Pitts. The two fell in love while still in college. In their youth, they were both ambitious dreamers. Both students at Virginia Commonwealth University, my father studied art history, having had a dream of being a museum curator or tour guide, while my mother studied nursing. Dad worked for campus security, and it was through his duties as an RA that he met my mother.

I never understood what attracted my mother to my father. In college, he had long hair, an attitude, and lots of denim, then again, it was the 1990s. He was a family man, even before he had one of his own. The way my dad took care of anybody that came into his life was unlike anything I'd ever before seen. Something about his natural way to simply make people *feel* was what made people so comfortable around him and it was this that I suspect made my mother so attracted to him.

Out of college, my mother began service in the United States Army reserves refueling aircrafts, eventually transitioning to employment with the local police department, and my father began working for the Virginia Department of Transportation, working to improve the transportation needs of the state of Virginia and striving to keep all those on the roads safe.

The image of my parents is what is reflected in me: two hard working people who've given all they had to their employers, only to receive blisters on their hands, pain in their backs and a meager paycheck. However, hearing them complain about bills at such a young age, didn't stop them from providing the most essential thing to their son; love.

The name "Tristan" came from the Brad Pitt movie *Legends of the Fall*, in which Brad Pitt played a long blonde haired war hero, plagued by disastrous events. Watching the movie together, my parents decided it was a beautiful name. As a child, I had the blonde hair of Brad Pitt, and most of my early years were spent running around shirtless just like a Brad Pitt film.

Essential to my early childhood was the emphasis on the growth of my imagination. I wasn't told how to grow up but rather was encouraged to create my own identity. My development hinged on sitting in the living room watching *Barney* or *Dragon Tales*, playing with Fisher Price pirate/cowboy playsets. While having massive battles between the pirates and cowboys that didn't determine the fate of the world like I thought they did, they certainly shaped mine.

Chapter 2

It's My Life

My prayer was that God would break me in the same way that Jesus was broken nearly 2,000 years before. I got out of the shower, and began putting my clothes on, watched a little TV, and then at 7:02 in the morning my cell phone rang. It was my dad.

—⁂—

My dad had this white, two door, 1995 Toyota tacoma truck, when I was growing up. I swear I thought that thing was God or at least made in heaven, because that truck seemed to run forever. Because the truck was a '95 model it was equipped with manual windows, a keyhole where you would place your key in to turn the passenger airbag off, and a tape player.

As dad worked longer for VDOT, his job location continued to change as his experience grew, so his commute became longer, and with this he decided the tape player was outdated, and that a CD player was needed in his truck if he was going to make the commute to northern Virginia. For hours, I remember my father working hard to install the system on his own. It was a project he knew he could accomplish. In between a few beers, in the middle of daylight, he got it done.

The next morning was foggy, and the roads wet from the rain the night before. In my hands was a piece of toast, smothered in butter and grape jelly, the usual. Dad was old enough to conquer the world, I was old enough to barely see over the dashboard of that old white truck. To this day, I can not remember where we were going, but on that morning, looking back, I found myself.

The year was 2000, and to my dad Bon Jovi never grew old, nor became irrelevant, so he ripped open the packaging on his new Bon Jovi "Crush" CD, and from the sound of the first guitar riff he seemed to be transported back to the days when he would play bass in a local band as a teen. My father was in his early thirties, I was five, but reflecting on it, I am having a hard time distinguishing who the child was.

Dad was so full of life, so undeterred from his dreams. What I am so thankful for is that he never taught me how to live, he simply lived and that was all I needed to see to know how I want to be. Everything he did, he did with passion and love, this was seen in the way a grown man unashamedly could still play the air guitar or air drums at a stop light and simply not care what he looked like to the car beside him.

The things that were close to him, were the things that he used his heart to prop up above the clouds. If he believed in something, he would give that thing or person all he had to make the situation better or the person happier. Randy James, my dad, became a shelter for people; a place people could go to entrust their deepest concerns.

On that same Bon Jovi album "Crush", there is a song called "It's My Life". The song is not just a Billboard Top 100 hit, but an anthem. No song resonates with the person I saw in my father's blue eyes that day. The beauty of the song doesn't come from the vocals, or the musical talent, but the meaning of the words and the message conveyed from it. The song is a challenge to live life while you still have life to live, the song is a requiem for those who've gone before us and have given so much of themselves to make this world better. It's a song for those who've been told to quit, but fight anyway.

If there is one thing that I have learned since hearing this song, sitting next to my dad all those years ago, it is this: life is fragile, and the moment you think it is secure and safe is the same moment, like a vase, it falls to the ground and breaks.

As a kid, you feel safe. Invincible. Unbreakable. However, that innocence is quickly taken back by the society we live in, the things children are exposed to and the way things simply are.

In 2001, my parents divorced, and I didn't understand why my dad wasn't at the house for Thanksgiving, or the reason why there was a man I wasn't too familiar with spending Christmas with my mother and I. I didn't understand at the time why my brother was a slightly different color than me, or why that same man held him and called him son, while he only called me "Tristan."

I saw my dad every-other weekend, which to a child, seems like an eternity. As the years progressed, and I grew older, the opportunity to see my dad was what caused me to study a lot harder in school. I thought if I did all of my school work well, he would be proud of me and then I could tell all of my friends in class that my dad was coming to pick me up!

At that age, when you see two people you love separated from each other and you don't understand "why", you feel helpless, but also it hurt a lot. Because every attempt to try and get my mom to go live with my dad again, so we could be "a family again", failed, which made the distance of traveling from house to house that much greater and the definition of a "home" foreign to me.

No matter what you are facing in your life, situations do not outlast the survivor. Meaning, no matter how painful whatever it is you are dealing with may be, the fact that you are reading this book is proof enough that you are running just a little faster than that which is chasing you, it is proof that you are surviving and that the pain is pushing you to higher heights! Because you are reading this book, you are a survivor, someone who decided to live life adventurously no matter the cost. Your pain isn't permanent, but it is for a purpose.

Despite the pain the divorce of my parents caused me throughout my childhood, I always clung to the memory of dad and I riding in his truck, not having a destination, listening to "It's My Life", barely being able to see over the dashboard. "It's My Life" wasn't just a song Jon Bon Jovi wrote about his own life, he wrote the song about my dad, he wrote the song about a hollywood movie star, a barber, an inner city teacher, a single mother. Jon Bon Jovi wrote this song about all of us, because life isn't meant to be lived by only one group of specific people, but by everyone before it's too late.

Chapter 3

Don't Sweat The Small Stuff

When we got to the hospital, we had no idea what to expect …

—⚬—

The stage was set, and in the seats looking up towards it were the most anxious group of sixth graders William Wetsel Middle School had ever seen. I was among them, and am still unsure of how fast my legs were shaking with nervousness as to how the new year as a middle schooler would begin. We were all rising 5th graders, and even though we were at "the bottom" again, we still felt like we were big stuff, as long as we could remember our locker combination.

Jim Sanderson, one of our guidance counselors, addressed us first. Before the principal, the teachers, or anyone else could say a word, Mr. Sanderson took to the only thing he knew how to do to calm down a new group of knee-knocking sixth graders: inspire them.

"I have two rules", he said.

"Number one: Don't Sweat The Small Stuff."

"Number two: Everything Is Small Stuff."

To understand the impact this had, you have to have a better conception of who Mr. Sanderson is. Meeting Mr. Sanderson for the first time, with his southern drawl, his beard, his flannel shirts on occasion, and his incredible sense of humor, I was unsure of why he was not touring with Jeff Foxworthy on the "Blue Collar Comedy Tour".

To an incoming sixth grader, he was the equivalent that aspirin is to a headache, a relief. They couldn't have had a more appropriate first speaker than him. So throughout his whole conversation with us he is making jokes about being shoved into lockers, being late for class, or eating the mystery meat in the cafeteria and then does a complete turn-around by ending on a serious note, imparting in me and others the greatest gift I've ever received.

There was never a time from sixth grade to eighth grade that I ever saw Jim Sanderson frustrated. Confused, yes, but never angry at anyone. This came from the personal convictions he held in his own heart. That each of us annoying runts had something to contribute to his walk with God, while also being a personal development to himself. No matter what came to him, he always greeted it with the mantra he preached:

"Don't Sweat The Small Stuff."

"Everything Is Small Stuff."

This outlook on life is the reason I saw him as one of the most successful men I've ever met. He didn't have the best job, that's because he worked with kids all day, and he wasn't paid thousands upon thousands of dollars, that's also because he worked with kids all day, but he confronted his problems and saw them as smaller than himself, which is what made him a conqueror and a victor over the things that bothered him.

In the seventh grade, I wanted to run for vice president of the school. My friend and "campaign manager", Ashton Weakley and I, wanted to have fun. We had a good chance in winning, as there was only one other person running, as long as we didn't joke around. Unfortunately, we decided that the main issues of my campaign would be the "hard pressing issue" facing our school of getting whole milk back into the cafeteria. In fact the slogan was, "A vote for Tristan is a vote for whole milk." Needless to say, we did not win.

"Don't sweat the small stuff."

"Everything is small stuff."

The following year against three other classmates. Ashton and I, both, knew that the odds would be stacked against us, because middle school is probably the greatest representation of national politics, it's cliquey, and because there were three other candidates running to be president of the school the votes were sure to be split among all of us. We shook hands and gave hugs, took tests and more tests. The life of middle school politicians is a crazy mix. We didn't allow the previous election to get us down, instead we used it to prosper us, and in eighth grade, I was elected as president of Wetsel Middle School. We could have just given up and decided that we simply would not be able to make it in middle school politics, however, we applied Mr. Sanderson's advice and kept going, the outcome was one of my happiest middle school memories.

Meanwhile, at home, we started facing things and terms that I didn't know how to define. Words like "unemployment" and "food stamps" came into my mothers vocabulary leaving me confused as to what was happening. My mother started saying "No" or "Maybe Santa will bring it" to my brother and I's requests for this thing or that thing. As more and more things disappeared from our house, it became more clear to me what was happening. My mother had been let go from her employer at the time, and for nearly a year searched for work while my brother and I saw the effects of having no income in the house.

I wanted so desperately for my mother to have the means she needed for us to be okay as a household. Many nights were spent in prayer asking God for my mother to find employment or listening to her cry alone in her room as she was distraught over how she would pay this bill or that one before that service would be cut off like the others.

It was hard for a twelve year old to understand the complexities of finding a job, and the nature of the economy in 2008, but for my family and many others, times weren't just tough, they were excruciating. My brother's father had left my mother, and now without any income my mother was expected to provide for two boys solely on her own, with the help of my father's child support check that he willingly gave her. Statistics show of the 8.1 million families living in poverty during the recession of 2008, 3.6 million of them were headed by a single mother.

During this time, I found solace in the scriptures, a true need for something when everything else was lacking. Before she was let go, my mother was the admissions director for a local nursing home. Having met my mother through the nursing home, as her father was a patient, Louise Campbell offered to come and hold a Bible lesson in our home each week to help our household get through the hard time we were having. My mother did not continue the Bible study after the first week, but in that Bible study with Ms. Louise everything began to make sense in my life.

Every Tuesday, we would meet at my mothers house for Bible study and snacks after I got off the school bus. It was such a joy to learn about the heroes of the Bible such as Noah, Joseph, Daniel. Ms. Louise opened my eyes to scriptures that began to give me hope, and made me believe that even in this trial there is a God who truly cares about the well being of my soul. She became to me like a grandmother, and

I her grandson. She began taking me to her place of worship and it was there that I learned the meaning of fellowship and community.

The first few meetings I went with her, I only had the Bible she had given me, other than that I only had a few pairs of good jeans and khakis, along with some sweaters that I would wear to every Sunday meeting. Ms. Louise told me not to worry about how I looked, so long as I continued to come and learn the truth that God loves all of His creation.

In the third Sunday of my attendance, Ms. Louise introduced me to one of the most loving couples. This man and woman, purchased for me three brand new dress shirts, and gave me an assortment of his personal ties, as well as a snazzy blazer to wear with my khakis. I felt like a million bucks. This act was one of the things that established for me the necessity to help others, along with the beauty of doing so.

In a time of great need, God drew near to me by using a sweet old lady to teach me about Him, while He used others to teach me what love actually was; an action.

"Don't sweat the small stuff."

"Everything is small stuff."

Trials come into our lives in order to do one thing, show our trials the greatness of the human spirit. No matter how big of a problem or predicament you think you are in, the reality is that you have been conditioned and created to be bigger and stronger than the things that are trying to get you to fall.

I am thankful Ms. Louise Campbell taught me about Noah, Joseph, and Daniel, because although they were great figures of the Bible, they only became great because of the thing tried to do them harm. I believe God placed Noah through the flood, not to teach Noah about floods, but to teach floods that there are some people you can not drown. I believe Joseph was placed into prison, not to learn about prisons, but to teach prisons that there are some people you can not keep bound. Finally, I believe God placed Daniel in the lions den, not to teach Daniel about the ferociousness of a lion, but to teach lions that there are some people you can not eat.

These heroes of the scriptures knew that they were bigger than their problems, and that the reason they were enduring the trial was to teach it and us that it was just something meant to be overcome.

All these years have passed since hearing those words as a nervous sixth grader:

"Don't sweat the small stuff."

However, now I finally understand it.

The reality is that no matter how many times other people have given up on your dreams, hang in there, you are going to meet a person far more important who can facilitate your greatest growth in order for that dream to come to pass! No matter how many times you have been told that you are not good enough, one day prince charming or cinderella will come storming by and will look you in the eyes and tell you they love you. You have far too much to offer the world to remain seated in mediocrity.

God has created you to do life big and because you've been equipped to slay dragons, and survive floods it's time that you realize that no matter what you are going through:

"Everything is small stuff."

Chapter 4

The Minister and MESA

Before this, for about nine months, dad complained of having chest pains. He had been going to the doctor to have tests done in order to find out if anything was wrong with him that doctors could treat then. EKGS, stress tests, ultrasounds, holter monitors, blood tests, all normal.

—∽—

In eighth grade, I started to lose touch with Ms. Louise, however, I still loved the material I learned from her, and I wanted to continue to grow in my relationship with God, as well as continue fellowship with a Christian community of believers. Down the road from the place we were living at the time was Fairview Christian Church. I had never been cause I had always been going on Sunday's with Ms. Louise. Because I still wanted to go and learn of the things God has planned for His children, I made an effort to find out more about the church.

As I was doing research over a span of time, as to when service times would be and how often they met a week, some ladies from the church brought cookies to our house during the Christmas season, something they did for all the houses in the immediate vicinity of the church. This act of kindness moved me so much and little did I know how much of an impact this church would make on the remainder of my life, as I devoured each bite of the snickerdoodles. I had to make up my mind as to whether or not these cookies were heavenly because of how delicious they were, or from the devil, himself, because they were going to go straight to my thighs.

That Sunday, there is not a set of words that can describe the simplicity and humility of the church. As you walk in the church foyer, there is nothing but a place to hang your coats and place your umbrellas, and a place to sign your name should you be a guest. The sanctuary was similarly quaint and quiet as the most elaborate thing in it was the painting of the Lord, Jesus Christ, which hung behind the pulpit.

Fairview was a country church. Located in the foothills of the Blue Ridge Mountains, Fairview wasn't trying to be a church that got caught up in how it looked but rather how's it parishioners developed in their relationship in the community and with God. At the helm of this church, was Rev. Tommy Lynn Palmer, and while the church had a quiet atmosphere, he certainly wasn't! Tommy's love for God, and the people under the sound of his voice is what gave his life meaning and made his voice boom and echo through the church.

Tommy Palmer was born on March 15, 1944, and it seemed he never grew old. I met him that fateful Sunday 2010. He strolled in with a cowboy hat, and a jean jacket, the Bible in hand. Noticing I was new he reached his hand out for mine, and shook it, telling me welcome, as he hugged and shook the hands of others while on his way back to his office. Fifteen minutes later, as the piano music began to play the call to worship, he reemerged from the back, his white hair that was underneath the cowboy hat now shined, and he was now in a priests robe, but his Bible never left his hand.

His preaching style was filled with stories from his personal life, showing us that he wasn't immune to pain, heartache, or trials just because he was a preacher. His scriptural knowledge was so profound as had to have quoted at least ten scriptures in each sermon. However, what impressed me most wasn't the fact he was a Biblical scholar, or could tell nice stories, the thing that stood out most to me about Rev. Tommy Palmer was that when it was time to preach he would step off of the elevated stage and begin delivering his sermon among the congregation. There would be times when he would walk up and down the aisles, while other times he would lean on the pews and have direct conversations with his congregants.

Seeing him lean on the pews, to me, sent a great message about this man's character, that message being he needed us, but more importantly he loved us. Tommy's messages were simple but challenging. His sermons never became tangled up in dogmatic ideas but rather would always express the love Christ has for those that follow Him through their service to others.

Understanding this, you start realize that Tommy's pulpit never was something that could be found in a church but rather it was found in the hearts of those he inspired. Tommy's pulpit was the community he served and the people he reached out to. He would write weekly newspaper columns in the local paper giving people hope for their troubled times, even if they didn't attend his church or church in general. Beyond this, he sponsored community breakfasts and, in true mountain tradition, apple butter festivals. Tommy's ministry was service, and his sermons were based around doing the works of Christ rather than just making noise.

While in the last semester of eighth grade, my family's financial situation worsened. Because of this, we were in jeopardy of losing our house. There wasn't any clarity as to what would happen, or where we would go. Our landlord, graciously let us stay until the summer of 2010, so we could continue to pursue options around the county or across the state in terms of finding a place to go.

Knowing that at any morning you woke up the electricity could be turned off because the bill went unpaid, or that the phone was disconnected and you couldn't call anyone to ask for their help was part of the fear that we dealt with the spring of 2010.

My mother, with a rare kidney disease, did the best she could not only trying to find stable employment to pay house expenses, but also to pay for her medical bills. There were times when the only thing in the cabinets to have for breakfast and dinner were cans of fruit. It wasn't through her fault that we were struggling, that we were in poverty. My brother and I wore shoes until holes began to form and sometimes longer than that until new ones could be purchased. Our clothes never fit us to form they were bigger, hand-me downs, thrift store bought.

Much of our time that spring was spent at the library, because other than DVD's, we couldn't pay for the television service to remain on. It was through this that I found myself getting farther lost in a world of books. My little brother, at this time 9 years old, who struggled with reading and grasping essential concepts of lessons taught in school, found his literacy skills getting stronger through the books he would read about presidents, wrestlers, and snakes.

Things continued to go the way they had the previous months, and in the summer of 2010, we were taken in by MESA, Madison Emergency Services Association. MESA was an organization that served the Madison community through it's community food bank and it's own thrift store, Connie's Thrift, MESA has worked since 1982 to develop emergency relief programs to help those in poverty in Madison county. One of the facets of MESA was the shelter that it provided in the form of apartments for those families that had fallen through the cracks and were close to being swallowed up. This shelter was called "Barbara's House", and for families in severe financial need, who met qualifications were brought in to live rent and bill free for a year in order to reestablish themselves and get back on their feet financially.

Barbara's House was where I began high school at. All throughout my school years, no one knew what my family was going through partly because I was too young to understand it all myself. As a freshman in highschool, it started to make all the sense in the world what we were facing. It was a hard transition to move into this new place, as well as start my first year in high school. High school produces all the awkward moments necessary for freshmen, but living in a place like Barbara's House where no visitors were allowed only residents made friendships harder to maintain as no one could come over to visit unless it was outside on the front porch where any of the other residents could take place in your conversations.

There were four other families that lived in Barbara's House, plus ours. There were eight kids total in the house and I was the oldest at 14. All of the families were headed by single mothers. My father was the only one of the eight kids there that was truly active in my life, whereas the other kids barely had any involvement from their fathers. Looking back on it, it shows me the importance of real men to step up and be fathers in the lives of their children. Not for the sake of anything but being a hero and champion for the dreams of their kids.

Because of this, one of the most influential people I met was through Barbara's House. Ms. Retha Alderton was like the grandmother of the house. Ms. Retha could cook! I learned a lot by just going downstairs to her apartment and watching her in the kitchen make miracles with what little she had. Ms. Retha was an incredible cook, and butter was the main ingredient, so you knew it was good. Watching her cook and eating her food was a way Ms. Retha could sneak in a few lessons about life. Ms. Retha taught me at her dinner table about the value of women and what treating a woman looked like.

Barbara's House was helping put our lives back together and for that I am forever grateful. It gave families who had been broken a second chance. However, with it, there came problems.

One of the most vivid things I can remember was waking up along with my brother one morning with red marks on my arms and having to go to school with the embarrassment of people asking me what they were. We weren't sure what it was. We didn't know if was some sort of rash or maybe even the chicken pox. The next morning, new red marks appeared on my arms as well as my legs and torso. After new marks continued to increase, and would show up only in the mornings after waking up, we did further research. The marks were not from any kind of skin reaction, but were bite marks. All apartments were infested with bedbugs. The old adage, "Don't let the bedbugs bite," had become the mark of our poverty.

To know that at any moment of the night a swarm of insects were crawling not only over me, but also my family and other families of the house, made me shiver as to why we were having to wake up to the purple streaks these bugs left on our bed sheets and the red bites they left on your arms as you itched at them for days. MESA tried several extermination attempts but because there were so many of them, if one survived they would multiply again, and be tracked into other apartments all over again.

I say this not to tell you the flaws of the place which so graciously kept us from the streets but to point out through our struggles, that despite the size of something so small as a bedbug our lives were changed by that little critter. If something so small can make this much of a difference, do you not think that someone like you, with your dreams, can make the same, if not greater, impact on the lives of others?

Aside from the bed bugs, being farther away from the church family that I had fostered was starting to upset me. I missed hearing Rev. Tommy's sermons and also just missed being with folks from the church who took care of me as if I was their own. Because of the stress of the financial situation, my mother and I started to develop an unhealthy relationship, and while I went to my dad's every other weekend to release that stress, I also relied on the church ladies to be there for me as well.

It was a few months after moving into Barbara's House, when I got a phone call from him Rev. Tommy. Tommy heard that our family had moved from our old house and asked how things were financially. Previously, he had helped through having the church donate funds to us to try to help pay for bills, and I assumed this was the reason he was asking, that he wanted to give me money for my family. He asked me different questions about God, Heaven and Hell, etc. which always became opportunities for him to teach me about the things of the Bible. Neither of my parents were very religious, in the respects to reading the Bible a lot, and knowing where this was or that was in the scriptures, so conversations like these with Tommy shaped my beliefs and goals for a future in ministry. He was the man who inspired my faith.

A few weeks before Thanksgiving 2010, I received another phone call from Rev. Tommy. He told us to come outside of Barbara's House, that he was there to see us. I rushed down the stairs and there he was, standing in front of his little pickup truck, with his signature cowboy hat and jean jacket on his body to keep his white hair and his body warm. Seeing his smile was warming enough.

"I have something for you all," he said.

And with that he reached into the back of his pickup truck and pulled out from the bed two large boxes of food. Snack foods like Nutrigrain Bars, applesauce, crackers, chips, pudding, as well as staples for a Thanksgiving dinner such as gallons of milk, boxes of stuffing, sweet potatoes, and of course turkey, lined each box to the brim.

"One more thing," he said.

He reached inside of his truck to pull out a plastic tub of cookies from the church, the same homemade cookies which was the act that inspired me to go to their church in the first place.

After giving us these things, he gave me the biggest hug and told me that no matter what happens in my life that God will always be present through it all. Thinking back this, it has become a mantra that I can't live without, because no matter how many times I've tried to focus my attention on things other than God, whether it be sports, relationships, video games, etc. He not once has given up on me.

The hardest thing about believing in God is remembering through all the pain that He still believes in you. When you realize that His love for you is unending, that because of His son, your mistakes are no longer mistakes but rather stepping stones which He uses to teach you how unbreakable you are, you begin to grow and find new meaning in life.

Out of our desire to serve Him and the faith that He is active in our lives, we find ourselves being risen from the pit to the palace, just like Joseph. It's out of God's love for His children that He blesses us, and also through that same love uses trials to teach us how strong we are in Him.

I believe that you WILL see the very thing you are praying or hoping for. Through fervent intercession the early church saw what they were praying for when Peter was freed from jail by the angel. (Acts 12) With that constant hope and determination miracles happen Keep praying, keep seeking.

My family could've been left out on the streets, but God saw our need and met it. We could've have gone hungry with nothing at all to eat, but even in the nights when we were eating cans of fruit, we were being sent a greater blessing through the ministry of Tommy Palmer, who understood churches do not have walls. We could've been a lot of things during that time, but the only thing that mattered was what God said we were going to be, which was His - blessed and loved.

The pain you are going through is the plan God has to show you how good He is.

Chapter 5

···

Ol' Blue Eyes

Seeing him seizing in a hospital bed I was starting to break at the edges and started crying for my hero.

He had found his kryptonite.

—❧—

My father had the sweetest blue eyes I've ever seen. Something about them just shone. Dad was the type of person who just knew how to make everything a little bit better. No matter what the situation was, no matter what you were going through, Randy James had a way to make you forget about it even if only for a second. Part of that was because of his goofy humor, but mainly because of his heart and love for just about everyone who came to him with cares and concerns.

Randy Lee James was born on December 22, 1969 to William and Nancy James. My grandparents had their work cut out for them if they were to raise him. From an early age my father had a certain genius about him, that reminiscing on it just makes you smile. His younger brother, Tony, was born four years after him, and the story goes that my dad would coax my uncle to get out of the bed at night when they were told to go to bed thus always getting Tony in trouble.

Dad developed talents and passions for things quickly. His love for art is what drove his early ideas of a potential career and also his field of study when he would get to college. In 1988, he graduated from Culpeper County High School and was accepted into Virginia Commonwealth University.

Being raised in Culpeper, which at the time was a small, rural town, Virginia Commonwealth University presented dad with the opportunity of being in the city of Richmond. It was a place where he grew exponentially into the man he later became for those who needed him most.

He was known as "Cat Scratch J", a name he earned because of his obsession with rock and roll music. One of dad's favorite musician's of the day was Ted Nugent, and it was his song "Cat Scratch Fever" that dad played loudly in Johnson Hall, during his days at VCU. Ted Nugent's guitar riffs gave my dad life it seemed. From Ted Nugent to Steve Vai, Kiss to Van Halen, the long mullet dad had in college went back and forth as his head bobbed to the rock and roll that got him through long nights of studying and many exams. His love of music was rooted in a background of playing bass in a high school band, and later a little electric guitar in college.

Aside from music, he started finding a love for film. He didn't want to act. He would be the first to tell you, that he could not act. However, it was bringing to life the words of others and giving others the spotlight that he enjoyed the most.

With a camera, dad would run around gorilla around the streets of Richmond, film all the life he saw. One of his roommates, Travis Stanberry, became the star of all their productions together.

Travis was shorter than dad by a few inches, and small in bone structure. However, Travis was most remembered by my dad for his impersonation of Charlton Heston's Moses. Imagine a little frame, going deep into his diaphragm to replicate Heston's booming voice:

"And Moses came down from the mountain."

Travis continued acting outside of college. Travis starred in episodes of Dawson's Creek, and also a few Lifetime movies. Travis sought after more roles to play in movies but found the most fulfilling role by becoming a husband and later a father to a son of his own.

Among photography, artistry, cinematography, he was also a collector. Dad started collecting baseball and football cards in college. He was an avid Pittsburgh Steelers, and Atlanta Braves fan and it was apparent in the countless T-Shirts and jerseys he had. In that collecting phase, he found a niche in comic books, an unseen, daring world where everything worked out for the good. He ended up collecting close to 800 comic books and 1,500+ sports cards.

Beyond what he was passionate about, dad worked hard as an intern for the Department of Transportation during his later years in college. As he gained work experience, VDOT also was the means that he paid his tuition. Seemingly, everything he did for the state of Virginia through his internship, helped develop a greater sense for his life of helping people get to where they needed to go.

My father's hands reflected those of someone who never gave up on his dreams. They were calloused and hard, serving as the proof of all the work he put into becoming the man others needed him to be. He always gave of himself. It didn't matter your relation to him, or what you had done for him. The only thing you had to do to receive his help and his concern was to be in need.

There were times in dad's life where he gave, and all people did was take. That, however, is the risk that comes with showing others love, yet to Randy James, that was the only way to heal others who needed it.

Something I learned from watching my dad firsthand was that change is inevitable. People you thought were close to you will profess their love for you one day, and turn on you in an instant. With the change in their attitude towards you, you too are changing.

Its amazing to see how much you can change: how much a single second, moment, year, or couple years can shift the character that you once encompassed. Looking back on the people we were but a short while ago only twists my thoughts to the ever looming future.

In dad's life, two of his marriages failed. The heartbreak he was left with enormous and the idea of starting over again was something that he was so confused about. He had given so much to my mother and to his second wife, that he wasn't sure what was left to give.

Writing this, I cannot help but think that every single event has been a brick carefully placed in the wall of our lives, that every instance has been a stepping stone for what comes next, and that the present may be the defining moment of what will build our fates, and the fates of those who come after us.

A few years after the his second marriage came to a close, dad found Tina Ragen. Tina was a go-getter, a woman at the top of her class. She was a natural entrepreneur who owned her own business, and not only owned her own business but was showing others around her how strong she was catering to her customers and by turning a profit.

She was a laborious worker, and this is what made her a compassionate boss, because as long as I can remember, whenever an employee of hers had an emergency preventing them coming into work, she stood up and took their place. Tina, like dad, had a servants heart, and together they made a strong bond of supporting each other, devotedly and unconditionally.

We stand atop the shoulders of giants, the pillars of a climbing ladder inspired by ideology, of the logistics contained within science and math, and of the imagination inspired by centuries of creative minds. Will we waste one moment? Will you waste one moment disregarding the opportunities given to you when so many would kill for the position of which you were born? Will you throw away all experiences that have molded my being because sometimes you feel uncomfortable with the work required to become great?

Too often we forget the past that shaped us, and forget that every single second of our life has led us to where we stand right now. I become easily discouraged by the negative thoughts that poison my mind, I give in to temptations, and I forget that I was meant to be something. Just like all of you were MEANT for something great, something inspirational.

We have all been put in positions where we can achieve more than we ever imagined, if we want it bad enough and for this reason my dad never stopped pursuing his dreams, despite the hollow words of his own conscious and of others. I saw him take it all in the changes, the negatives, and in response radiate greatness.

Dad understood what he had found in his first two marriages: heartbreak. However, had he stopped there and allowed it to be the end of his story, he never would have found Tina Ragen, a woman who was his equal, his support, his rib. He went through heartbreak to be positioned to find the joy in the miracle she was in his life.

Just like my father, I will never forget who I was or who I am, and I will never discontinue my "polite" disposition. Most of all, I will never stop believing in the people who no longer believe in themselves, who don't realize that sometimes all you need is a simple spark to ignite a lifetime of dedication, who don't yet see that they have a fire within them. I am a product of that insignificant spark, I am a product of the dreams my father was told to give up on.

You can be great despite your past, and despite what others think of you.

It is in your fate.

Tina lived in Spotsylvania, which from where I lived was an hour away. When dad moved in with Tina, he would drive, every other weekend, an hour to pick me up on Friday and hour to take me back on Sunday because he was that committed to being a father. To him, distance didn't matter. The miles that he had to drive he could afford to lose, but the time spent creating a bond with his son was something he could not.

I can't think of any moments that were the most fulfilling in my life than the ones spent with him on the weekends. Dad structured weekends like no other. His passion for learning fueled what we did. From trips to Washington D.C. to see monuments and museums, to laying on the couch together and watching the history channel he made it a priority to present material to me which would engage me to see the world in as many perspectives as possible.

Randy James was never content with being stagnant, to him there was nothing that was completely absolute. He believed in principles to be a foundation, however, for him, since life was always moving and changing so to should our ideas and conceptions change also. I believe that's what makes his parenting model so exceptional. I am nineteen years old, as I am writing this, and not once did my father ever tell me how to do something. He just lived, and I was blessed to be able to see him do so.

In life, the greatest ways of learning aren't through lectures or mandatory reading, but rather through constant observation and examination of oneself can one find true meaning and fulfillment. Beyond examining oneself, the tool that makes the most successful people successful is their ability to discern the actions of others.

The important thing to remember is that you will never be someone else. As hard as you try, as dutiful as you are, you will never become or achieve the exact same life that someone else has. I used to think that I wanted to be my dad, but as hard as I tried to obtain this idea of who my father was I always failed. When I accepted that I would only be successful if I was my best self rather than an imitation of my father I started to see success.

Imitation is never attainable, as you will always be your first and last name and never anyone elses. Besides, why would you want to be someone's copy? You've been created to be bolder, stronger, wiser!

You've been created to be you!

Aside from learning with dad, I was always eating with dad. He never cooked, but Hardees sure did! Every Saturday morning we would go to Hardees for breakfast, and back for dinner. It was the life. It's not that didn't know how to cook, he just liked Hardees a lot more. I am not sure how he didn't come to own that Hardees, with as much revenue that he gave them they should've at least placed his picture on the wall.

Football was also a big part of the time together. Sundays were spent in bed watching his Steelers and my Raiders, while huddled around the computer as we watched how our fantasy teams did for the day. He competed in a league with some of his coworkers, and they really didn't know what they were competing for considering they were not betting money in this league, for my sake.

One day at work, dad's friend Craig found an old boot in his office, and we've been competing for that dirty thing ever since. It became our trophy. Neither dad, nor I, ever won the boot and that was possibly a good thing. The rumor was that it smelled awful, and I can imagine why, Craig's feet were nasty. I think we started intentionally picking bad players to be on our fantasy team to ensure that we were not going to win that smelly thing and that it would stay with Craig.

Football was something we could disagree upon and have fun competing against each other with. It didn't take much to get a conversation going about Super Bowl predictions, or who would be traded during the offseason. We would crunch statistics and numbers to see who were the top performers on each team, and it felt like we should be in a suit and tie standing on the sidelines as reporters or owners with as much as we knew about almost every team in the NFL.

My dad never got old. That man would never stop playing video games. He stayed up to date with all the latest games and game systems, and enjoyed every minute of playing them. His nightly ritual would include watching TV with me until I fell asleep, and then going back to play games on his computer while downing a few beers.

It was his time to be by himself. Tina would already be in bed, and I fast asleep on the couch, so this was his time to bring out the inner nerd in him by fighting dragons, witches, and all things evil. He loved games where he could become a knight, or wizard and fight against things that were larger than life. I think it had to do with not only the entertainment of it all but the idea that he was fighting against something so evil and that he would slay that which was trying to kill him and his family.

Shortly before I was born, my dad's mother was diagnosed with pancreatic cancer. This news came as a shock to them as they didn't expect something like this to happen to a woman who was always healthy. My grandmother got very, very sick in her battle. However, there with her through it all was dad.

No one can expect, or be prepared for the moment you learn someone you love is fighting a losing battle. However, dad didn't see the words "losing battle", he saw the word "fighting." He bended over backwards for his mother during this time. He would cook for her and bring food to her in the hospital. He would clean the house while she was away, so when she came back it would be a completely different place. He showed her love when she needed it most.

My grandmother fought hard. She was a schoolteacher, so if anyone knew how to be patient during a stressful time it was her. She was constantly trying to improve, trying to fight a little harder to survive and beat the cancer that was trying to take her life, however, through it all dad was there in her corner just trying to comfort her and let her know that no matter how hard or fast she was trying to accomplish it was not important, but her persistence was.

Dad's support, truly, I believe, is what got my grandmother through it. She was given a hard battle but he fought with her and stayed by her side until the fight was won. Through her pain, her sadness, her moments of doubt he was there to reassure her that everything was working together for her good, that everything was going to be alright because he was there and was not going to leave her.

Despite all the odds in her battle with one of the most irrepressible forms of cancer, my grandmother won her battle, and is still around to tell her story, because my dad stayed with her to help slay the dragon which threatened her, just like those video games he would play on the computer, while supporting her until she was safe.

If you have never met my father, the Randy James I came to know, after his college days started getting flat tops instead of letting his hair grow out, started wearing T-Shirts instead of collared shirts, and started realizing his legs were way too hairy to wear shorts in public, so he wore a lot of jeans. His physique changed to a little round Pooh-Bear belly. When he walked, he walked with a little waddle, as if he was a duck. Dad was never amiss to how he looked, he just didn't care. The only wardrobe requirement he had and followed was to never wear anything red. He hated the color red.

Dad strived to be the best. He didn't know exactly how he would achieve everything he wanted in his life, but he knew that he would be the last person in the room to quit. His goals were clear, be the best person he could be in every area of his life. Being the best included making strides in his labor.

Dad worked his way through the ranks of VDOT, attaining the knowledge and skills to become a bridge safety inspector, yet this was a man who did not have an engineering degree but rather an art history degree.

To dad, life wasn't about how much money you could make or how much fame you could obtain but rather how content you were with yourself when you looked in the mirror at the end of each day.

Part of this contentment, came with proving the people who doubted him wrong. If someone in his life told him that there was no way it could be done, he would work at it until it was done.

In life, if you do not try something that people say is impossible then it always will be.

If you try it and fail, so what? People expected you to fail, but if what if you try and succeed?

The reality is that no one who ever become anything in this world became successful by doing nothing. They took risks, sweat and bled, until they became and achieved that which they dreamed of. Regular people become super heroes by giving all of themselves to something wholeheartedly.

That was my father.

A man who did not quit, simply because it got hard or uncomfortable.

You deserve to live the life you dream of, but like my father, you must resolve to live a life undeterred. The only voice you should listen to when determining if your dream is worthy of chasing is your own. No one knows how inspired you are, except for yourself.

When you allow the voices of others to crowd your mind, you give them power to run your life, to control how much you give to your dream. You become their puppet.

You were created to be more than a marionette on a string.

You were brought into this world to be:

The next President of the United States.

The next A-List actor.

The next New York times best seller.

The next Super Bowl MVP.

The next CEO of a Fortune 500 company.

The next Ms. Universe.

The world is chalked full of opportunities that no one else will take because they are too timid, too shy, too scared of being successful, but YOU? You know that you need to go after everything head first. You know that success is your birthright, otherwise, you wouldn't be reading this book still.

You've made the conscious decision that your life is more than just working a J.O.B. You've determined that you will no longer live your life "Just Over Broke" but rather you've seen that there is opportunity that others are passing up on so that they can be average.

You weren't built to be average or have a small impact.

You were created to have an impact as large as the world, and help others with your reach!

However, you will only go as far as you believe you will!

If you think that because you have limited resources compared to other people who've gone before you that means you're not able to accomplish your dreams, you're lying to yourself. If you think that your talents don't match up to the people at the top of your craft, and that is a reason to give up, you're wrong.

Stop comparing yourself to others, and rather be the best you! If you choose to work on yourself by looking only at your own reflection and not the reflection of others, I promise you that you will see the results you desire, because you no longer are working to obtain a goal that someone else has already obtained.

One of my dad's favorite actors was Jim Carrey, and a story I always remember dad vividly teaching me was of how Jim Carrey broke into the acting business. To him, it made sense to tell this story, to him I'm sure he thought it should be taught to every child in the world.

In 1985, no one knew who Jim Carrey was.

Jim was only 23 years old at the time.

He had dropped out of high school at 16 to pursue his career as an actor and comedian. Rather than having the success he thought he would have from the get-go, Jim Carrey instead became broke, poor, and depressed because he wasn't successful. With no educational background, he was either going to sink or swim. He had dedicated himself completely to acting and should he fail, he wouldn't have much to stand on afterwards.

In 1990, Jim wrote himself a check for $10 million dollars, and dated it for Thanksgiving of 1995. By signing this check to himself, he was visualizing his success, and gave himself five years to accomplish it. He placed the check in his wallet, and went to every audition, and casting call he could.

Though the check started to get worn, and tattered, he would pull it out and look at it every day. Before 1995, Carrey landed one of the lead roles in "Dumb and Dumber", and since then has been making millions on every film ever since.

Everyone now knows who Jim Carrey is, and his films are what cause so many of us to have joy in our darkest times, however, many of you reading this did not know the story of the check. Jim Carrey's success is proof that life is not about what people tell you is your destiny, but rather your destiny is solely based in what you desire and work hard to achieve.

My dad was the man who taught me this firsthand, time and time again. Whenever it seemed like life had knocked him down for good, through his failed marriages, or personal difficulties he always clawed and crawled back to his feet to fight again, not only for himself, but for those he wanted to give the world to.

What do you wish to achieve?

I want you to use the rest of the space on this page to write down where you want to be in ten years.

When you read the last chapter of my words in this book, come back and read yours, then conquer!

Like Jim Carrey you have to make the effort to see yourself and do things that support your dream, and like my father, you have to have the determination that you will not quit until you see the thing, despite all the things that knock you down.

At the very beginning of this chapter, I talked about my dad's blue eyes. Dad's eyes were the way you could tell what was wrong with him. They always had a certain reflection when he was sad, and a different reflection when he was happy. However, there was never a time when compassion, that will to be someone people could count on, left his eyes.

And to you, the reader, if you wish to see your dreams come true, like "Ol' Blue Eyes", you must never forget to reach out a hand to those around you, because they too are fighting the same uphill battle.

"SOMETHINGS NEVER CHANGE."

"OL' BLUE EYES."

"TINA RAGEN MADE DAD SMILE BRIGHTER
THAN I'D EVER SEEN HIM SMILE."

MR. MCSHERRY LIVED LIFE IN THE FACE OF SORROW. HE
WAS GREATER THAN THE CANCER THAT TOOK HIM.

"THE PICTURE LANE COLORED SO MANY YEARS
AGO WAS THE MASTERPIECE OF HIS LIFE ..."

REVEREND TOMMY PALMER WITH HIS ICONIC
JEAN JACKET AND COWBOY HAT.

KAITLIN'S NICKNAME IN HIGH SCHOOL WAS FLEE, BUT NO
MATTER HOW SMALL SHE WAS SHE ALWAYS DID GREAT THINGS!

SERVING AS AN INTERN WITH JOEL OSTEEN, I WAS BLESSED
BY GOD TO BE ABLE TO LEARN FROM HIM. (LEFT) MY BEST
FRIEND, TYLER KEMP, AND DUO PARTNER FOR THREE OF THE
MOST SUCCESSFUL YEARS OF MY LIFE. (TOP RIGHT) BEING
AWARDED THE BOYS AND GIRLS CLUB YOUTH OF THE YEAR
WAS AN HONOR THAT I HOLD VERY HIGHLY (BOTTOM RIGHT)

Chapter 6

"Code Blue, Medical ICU"

In the darkness of my bedroom red digits began to flash, the alarm clock sounded. I stumbled out of bed to begin getting ready for school. My desk lamp was on from the night before and the calendar read, April 22, 2011, "Good Friday". The idea that a god would have so much love for those who turned their back on him, by giving all of himself, always amazed me.

We are all guilty of making mistakes in our lives, but the Easter story is one that gives great joy. It's the story of Jesus conquering all the things we couldn't on our own through his crucifixion, for our sake, despite all the mistakes we could make in our lives. Through His death, the Scriptures tell us that we find the peace that Jesus completed the work and because of this sin and our failures should no longer hold dominion in our lives.

Obviously the most redeeming part of the Easter story is Jesus' resurrection, and His triumph over death. This resurrection is what assures us that we too can have victory over the dead things in our life, because we are also reminded that the same power that raised Jesus from the dead is in us.

(Romans 8:11) It this then, that is what we as believers should hold onto in times of great peril, and distress, as no matter whatever is dead in our lives, whether it is our finances, a relationship, or a dream, God has promised us that through our belief it shall be resurrected due to the power of Christ in our lives.

The whole week leading up to Good Friday is known as Holy Week. I had made the decision that I would spend the week studying each of the passages and anecdotes associated with that day in order to prepare for Easter that Sunday. My prayer life that week was centered on asking God to lead me in the footsteps of Jesus Christ that week, so that I could have a better understanding of His love for us, and ultimately understand His strength.

Easter weekend, 2011, was a weekend I would be spending with my dad. He would be picking me up on Friday and taking me back to Spotsylvania, to spend Easter with himself, and Tina, who he had just married on March 23, 2011.

I think to dad, marrying Tina Ragen was his greatest achievement. In her, he had found someone he could relate with in ways he had not been able to with anyone else. In her, he had found a woman who was not only successful in her own life, but also contributed to his own success in ways his parents, mentors, and friends never had. Her love for him was infinite, and his love for her was undying. For seven years they lived together before dad finally decided during Christmas of 2010 to ask her for her hand in marriage. This was his crowning moment, what I think he was fighting for so hard.

Nevertheless, he was going to pick me up after school on Friday like he would every other weekend. It was my second semester of my freshman year of high school, and we were still living in MESA. That morning I had rolled out of bed when my alarm rang at 5:00 am, and read the passages that were parallel with Good Friday.

After doing my daily, reading that morning I got in the shower to begin the rest of my day. I remember to this day, being caught up in the feeling of needing to pray. My prayer was that God would break me in the same way that Jesus was broken nearly 2,000 years before. I got out of the shower, and began putting my clothes on, watched a little TV, and then at 7:02 in the morning my cell phone rang. It was my dad.

I got out of the chair I was watching TV in, and answered the phone.

"Hey, dad!"

Except on the other line, it wasn't my father, it was Tina. She sounded distraught and anxious.

"Honey, your dad woke up this morning and he just fell down. He is in the Emergency Room at Spotsylvania Medical Center. I think you need to get here right away."

I remember feeling so calm on the phone with her when she was telling me all of this. I told her that I would be on my way as soon as possible and that somehow we would make it through this. All of us.

After getting off the phone with her the only images that flood into my mind after that was how slowly I sat back down into that chair, and then any feeling of calm was overshadowed by the overflowing of tears, as I just sat in my room and whailed at what I had just heard.

My father, the man who had taught me the most about life, had been hospitalized, and at this point when we got to the hospital we had no idea what to expect. We did not know his condition nor what the outlook was on if he would make it through or not. As soon as I got to the hospital I rushed to meet Tina. She had told me that doctors said dad suffered from cardiac arrest.

Before this, for about nine months, dad complained of having chest pains. He had been going to the doctor to have tests done in order to find out if anything was wrong with him that doctors could treat then. EKGS, stress tests, ultrasounds, holter monitors, blood tests, all normal.

My father had went through a gamut of testing and doctors had found nothing wrong with him.

Fast forward to April 22, 2011 and he is laying in a hospital bed.

We waited in the lobby for nearly two hours before we could go back and see him, and his physician did not tell us what we would see of my father when as four of us were only allowed to go back. Among the four that went back were his father, brother, wife, and his fifteen year old son, me.

Walking through the doors to see him, I was filled with anxiety. I was expecting to walk back and see my dad sitting up in a hospital bed, with those same shining blue eyes, that same big smile, to tell us everything was going to be alright.

As we were lead into his room I saw my dad laying in the bed, tubes down his throat and nose. Every few seconds he would shake, while his eyelids would open and his eyes roll back into his head. The nurse assured us that he was receiving medicine for the epileptic tremors he was having, but even with that assurance seeing my dad like that destroyed me.

Seeing him seizing in a hospital bed I was starting to break at the edges and started crying for my hero.

He had found his kryptonite. The man I had counted on for so long to be my rock, my guide, my inspiration but most importantly and simply he was my dad.

Doctors came to us about thirty minutes after we had saw him and told us that they would like our permission to medivac him to the University of Mary Washington Hospital, in order to perform a procedure called "therapeutic hypothermia". The goal of the procedure was to bring dad's body temperature low enough to preserve any of his organs from any further damage then they initially received.

When his heart stopped early that morning during his first episode of cardiac arrest, doctors were concerned that during that time my father's brain and other organs didn't receive enough blood. We knew it would be an uphill battle, and that because of the time it took to resuscitate him that morning lying on the bedroom floor that his brain had taken damage. Therefore, this procedure was to ensure that his organs would be kept safe as well as reduce any swelling around them.

Seeing dad's bed rolled out onto the helicopter pad and then lifted up onto the helicopter, all I could picture was my dad actually flying like the superhero I always thought he was, I didn't think of him being sick or on his death bed, but rather I saw this as yet another opportunity for him to teach me one more time about life.

When the helicopter arrived at Mary Washington around noon, he was taken into a room in the medical intensive care unit, and they started the treatment. We were allowed to come back around 1:30 or so, and when we were given the OK to come back, we had to use a telephone to phone the nursing station and tell them who we were in order to be taken back to see him. There I saw my dad much calmer than I had previously seen him. He no longer was seizing, as the medicine had started to work and run it's course. Although, he still shook as his they were constantly lowering his body temperature as part of the process. I can still see his face, eyes closed, oxygen mask on, with tubes down his nose and throat, mildly shaking from the cold. I didn't know which was worse. Seeing him seizing out of our control or seeing him shivering because of something we decided was best for him.

Countless people came to see him that Friday, and we decided to meet with them in the waiting room. Sitting there seeing so many people come through to talk to us and tell us they were supporting us, it all felt so surreal. I was supposed to be sitting with him at his house, and we would be watching TV, while he cracked jokes and told me stories about this thing or that. However, everything was like a whirlwind, and instead we found ourselves in a hospital ten minutes from his home, sitting and praying with everyone who came through, hoping he would pull through.

Around 4:00 that Friday, we heard over the intercom in the waiting room:

"Code blue, medical ICU."

It was repeated several times in order to alert any available nurses to return to the ICU and help the patient who had slipped into code blue. Code blue is a medical term that refers to a patient entering into cardiac arrest. All of us in the waiting room, now at least 20 people there for dad, looked at each other and said there was no way it could be him. He was resting so peacefully when we saw him a few hours before, and the idea of him going into another episode of cardiac arrest was completely foreign to us because it didn't fit the happy ending we wanted.

I'll never forget Tina and I rushing out of the waiting room to the doors of the medical ICU, picking up the phone on the outside and calling the nursing station. The locked doors opened and a nurse came to meet us in the hallway. Picture a man's new wife of nearly a month, and his 15 year old son, standing in the doorway of the medical intensive care unit hearing from a nurse:

"We've been trying to resuscitate him for almost 20 minutes but he is not responding."

It was with those words that my world started falling around me, and began breaking.

That one sentence still to this day haunts my nightmares.

After hearing that I ran to the chapel, and just started yelling at God. I had never been so angry at Him before. He had taken my father from me, and I was prepared to let Him know exactly how I felt. My body became exhausted from the flood of emotions and I sat down in one of the pews that was there in the chapel and started praying.

It was in that moment that my phone vibrated and I received a text from a girl from my school asking me if I had heard that Tommy died. I responded, asking what happened to Tommy Foster, a kid we went to school with. She sent a message back saying, not Tommy Foster, but Tommy Palmer. My beloved pastor, Tommy Palmer, the minister who taught me all about Christ, while showing me what God's love was all about, had died that morning from a heart attack.

My anger swelled again. In one day, God took my pastor and my father. I told God that I would serve Him, if He brought my father back. The classic, servanthood for a blessing exchange that so many people make. That was when it all started to make sense to me. It was in that moment that I remembered my prayer from the morning.

"...break me in the same way that Jesus was broken nearly 2,000 years before."

Before my eyes I was witnessing the crucifixion of my life, so to speak. I was feeling only a sample of the pain Jesus was feeling all those years ago. Now, at only 15 years old, I started to realize that not only was my pastor taken from me but also my father.

Seeing the correlation to these two being taken from me, I realize it was to prepare me for something greater. A pastor's duty is to teach the word of God to His congregants, and a father's duty is to reinforce that through his protection and showing of love to His children. By losing my father and my pastor, two of my greatest mentors, it was all to show me how much more God could give to me by being both of those roles for me in my life. I would became totally dependent on God, after this day, and find myself going to Him with everything. I started to feel as though God was right there through it all, that's because He was.

Opening up the large Bible that was on the podium in the chapel, I read aloud in the empty room.

"If ye then, being evil, know how to give good gifts unto your children, how much more shall your Father which is in heaven give good things to them that ask him?"

I saw through that scripture, that if God was going to remove something from your life, He was going to put in it's place things that would lead you to your greater divine destiny. God never gives big obstacles unless He uses them to be big opportunities for people to learn more about Him and His plans for their life.

After reading that passage, someone came in the chapel and told me they revived my dad and that I could go back and see him. I walked back to his room and just sat with him. Four more times that weekend, he would go through cardiac arrest episodes, and slip into a coma from the sedative drugs they gave him.

The hardest thing about seeing my dad in a coma, wasn't the fact that he was in a coma, but the image of nurses taking hold of the sheets underneath him in order to reposition his lifeless body. Here was the man that I saw the most strength in just being tossed around. This is one of the images that comes back into my mind daily.

For two weeks he laid in a coma. I remember sitting in his room with him everyday, but specifically on May 5th. It would be the last night I'd ever hold his hand, and sitting there I just watched him. I stared for what seemed like hours.

The next morning, May 6, 2011, after laying in a coma for nearly two weeks he was declared brain dead. He was 42. I replay those two weeks in my head everyday it seems; the conversations leading up to it, holding his hand and being by his bedside every waking minute, the prayers, the love from family and friends, the salty cafeteria food.

I remember it all like it happened today. And I just remember sitting there in his hospital room, looking on from a distance and realizing that life is like artwork. Sometimes you have to step farther back to appreciate it.

I had people tell me at the funeral, and at the viewing, "In time, things will get better." I find that three years later, I only miss him more. I miss the phone ringing around 5:00 PM everyday after school, just so we could talk about the days events. I miss the rides down the road in his truck whether listening to music, or laughing our heads off hysterically at each others jokes. I miss going to Hardee's every Saturday/Sunday morning I was with him to get breakfast, because even though he knew how to cook he hated it. I miss getting up next to him in bed, to watch a movie, football, or the history channel. I was always learning around him.

He never told me what to do; he just lived, and I was blessed to be able to watch him do it.

For the past few years I've had a bag packed with two pairs of clothes and two pairs of socks, waiting for him to pick me up for a weekend adventure. I've sat by the phone for the past few years waiting for it to ring so I could talk to him about the day, and hear him say, "I love you." I've lived the past few years as if I was dreaming, and that my father really wasn't dead - he was just away for awhile.

Unfortunately, the truth of it all is that he is gone; and for the past few years, I have spent most of my days talking to a stone that bears his name, but doesn't talk back. What has been only a few years, has felt like an eternity; the days seem longer, the months harder.

I spent 15 years with one of the most loving men I will ever meet. I owe him everything, and no matter how much pain I know it would cause me, I would do it all again. For all the joy, peace, strength, faith and love he brought to my life, I am thankful. I am the man I am today, because he loved me.

I've found the hardest thing about growing up is looking in the mirror and seeing that with each passing day I am beginning to look more like the man I miss the most. My hair recedes in the same place, his ears are on the side of my head, his strong jaw line is what mine replicates and from laying on his chest as a baby, his heart is what taught mine to beat.

I'm 19 years old, writing this and for four years since his death, I haven't heard my father's obnoxious singing voice among the "Happy birthday's". I wish so much for my dad to be here, to watch me as I go about life, to meet the people who mean the world to me, to hug me and tell me he loves me and is proud of me. I would give anything for him to come home late on a wintry Virginia night from his job with VDOT pushing snow, only to watch him open up a beer, sit down on the couch, and hear him make some comment about the Hannah Montana movie I'm watching.

I replay those same images again, and again in my head everyday.

And when I wake up tomorrow, I'll know I'll be one day closer to seeing my dad again.

Chapter 7

The Boss

When walked into room 203, one spring day in 2011, before dad was ever in the hospital, I had no idea what I was getting myself into. Honestly, I joined our high school forensics team on a whim, and also as an attempt to impress a girl who I had a crush on, who was on the team. The forensics I had stumbled into was not the CSI stuff you see on TV, but rather a form of acting in which performers would take a ten minute monologue, rehearse it, then perform it at a competition. Learning that I would have to wake up at 5:00 AM every Saturday, spend most of the day with people I didn't really like, and on top of that, learning I would have to wear a suit to every single competition, I didn't last long.

In fact, my freshman year, I only competed in one tournament, in which my duo partner and I qualified for the Virginia High School League State tournament. Chance had it that dad was getting married the same day as the state tournament, therefore I didn't have to compete. I was thrilled.

A month later dad passed away, and by the time I had got back to school after the funeral and a few days of reflection, the forensics coach asked to meet with me. I thought he was going to lecture me about not being at the practices and I would have to explain to him that my dad died. However, I had to do none of that. He already knew, and beyond knowing about my father's death, he knew about my family's financial situation. In this meeting, he told me that he wanted me to travel with the team to CFL nationals, and that he would pay for my trip. A weekend of fun in Washington D.C., all expenses paid? I was hooked!

The forensics coach was a man by the name of Donald Hitt. He spoke with a slight southern drawl, but that was because he went to college in Georgia, and as he described the country hicks messed him up. Mr. Hitt was originally born and raised in Culpeper, Virginia. He earned his bachelors degree from Piedmont College in Georgia, and later obtained a masters degree in curriculum and instruction from Longwood University in Virginia.

I always had the highest respect for Mr. Hitt. He was someone I reverently feared, since the day I met him, not because he was scary, but because of his vast accomplishments. When you walked into Mr. Hitt's room you would see trophies lining shelves that were built around the walls, and trophies that didn't fit on the overhead shelves were kept on the top of bookcases, and then trophies that didn't fit on the top of the bookcases were kept in the back of the room, while trophies that were too old were kept in the school's attic. Prior to me joining the program, he had won 14 state championships in forensics, and 3 for his theater productions. As a freshman to see all of that stuff, you can only be left in awe.

Mr. Hitt started coaching me and grooming me for success the minute I walked into the door. His tips on how to portray this character or that character no doubt led me to having success. His coaching was what caused me to become a great actor and performer, as well as orator and debater. When no one else believed in me, you might as well went to Mr. Hitt's room because that's where I would be, as he stood in my corner all four years of high school.

The second semester of my sophomore year, I never would've imagined that my duo partner and I would qualify for the national tournament but we did and we did because we won our first state tournament. I don't think Mr. Hitt could've been any more proud.

He had a few rough transition years before, my duo partner, Ty and I entered the program. He had lost all of his talented seniors, including a national finalist, and was trying to rebuild from the ground up. In Ty and I, I think he saw the future. I think he saw everything what this program was about to become. He made Ty and I almost the face of the program, and we returned everything back to him through winning first place at nearly every tournament we went to that year.

In forensics, the use of props and costumes is not allowed, and so the standard attire is a black suit. I didn't have enough money to afford a suit, and so I wore a blazer, with khakis. Mr. Hitt got me out of class one day and asked me to come to his room.

That year, the national tournament would be in Baltimore, Maryland. He told me that he understood how much my family was struggling financially, and that finances shouldn't be a reason that I do not compete at the national tournament that year. He simply looked me in the eyes and told me that he was going to pay for it, and make sure I got there. On top of that, Mr. Hitt told me that I wouldn't need to wear my blazer and khakis to the national tournament, because he was going to take me to the store a few weeks before the tournament and buy me a suit. I've never been more grateful in my life.

That was on top of all the times he waited outside of the school bus before we would go to competitions to hand me $20 to make sure I had money to eat dinner and lunch with. In at least every competition year, which started in September and went until June of the following year, there were at least 15 tournaments that we would compete at, including nationals, and I competed in the program for three full years.

If you do the math, he gave me at least $300 every year, in order to make sure I was fed. He was dedicated to making sure that while I was under his care that I was receiving the most adequate support I could, which included feeding me and putting the suit that I competed in on my back.

The dress shoes had never been worn before: genuine black leather, and tags still hanging from the side. I had barely known the man who gave them to me for more than a year, but that did not stop him from providing a gift that has been the foundation of my well being, and the cornerstone of my soul.

When I opened that box and saw those shoes laying inside, I couldn't help but cry. Those shoes have since walked through several high schools in Virginia and also in high schools nationally. The shoes have been on stage in several of our high school drama productions, and in final rounds at VHSL state forensics and debate competitions. The simple decision of walking into room 203, Mr. Hitt's room, has changed my life in more ways than I could ever describe, but the marks on the shoes tell the entire story.

Everyone says that we truly may not know a person until "we walk a mile in his shoes." Competing in forensics, and being the lead role in the three theater productions I was eligible for, allowed me that opportunity. Participating in the theatre and forensics taught me to see the world with a clearer focus. I played dramatic roles that helped peers with abuse and comedic roles that made my peers laugh at my zany antics. To that end, my director, my coach, "the boss", Mr. Hitt, taught me to walk with dignity and finesse in the face of personal hardship and in times of joy. I believe that is why these shoes that he has given me have traveled with me through the successes and defeats.

My greatest successes and multitudes of opportunities have come through the activities he coached me in. I loved the recognition, the medals, and the trophies but I realize that without the opportunity afforded me by Mr. Hitt I could not have accomplished these special feats in my life. He made me proud to represent my school, my team, and the Virginia High School League, Virginia Catholic Forensics League, and as a National Speech and Debate Association: Virginia Chapter as a state champion.

Because of him, I became a 7x state champion, winning three state championships from the Virginia High School League, three state championships from the Virginia Catholic Forensics League, and one state championship from the National Speech and Debate Association: Virginia Chapter. I broke our high school's record for most forensics points, which is calculated by the accumulation of rankings one is given during a performance, and I became the first student from our high school to win the National Speech and Debate Association: Virginia Chapter "Student of the Year" award.

When I joined Mr. Hitt's program the beginning of my freshman year, I would not have thought that I would be as successful as I was. Aside from the trophies and medals, the things that will fade away, the relationships I fostered through it became bonds that I believe will never be broken.

The heartache caused by my father's death, no longer stings as much, as forensics and drama became outlets; providing me with the experience of making others feel. Forensics and theater allowed me to look deeper into my past and my own soul, through using the talents and gifts given to me by God.

My senior year of high school, I laced my shoes one last time for the national tournament. For years, I had been chasing a national championship. My senior year the national tournament was held in Chicago, and Mr. Hitt got really sick. He was not going to be traveling with us. I fought and clawed, tooth and nail that tournament, because I wanted to win for him. If I did nothing else, that was what I strived for.

With the shoes he gave me, I walked across the stage to receive the seventh place trophy. I had finished seventh out of two hundred other kids. It was my best showing at the national tournament in all my years of forensics, and it was all for him.

I always called Mr. Hitt "the boss", mainly because if he told you something and you executed it the way he told you to, then you would see the tangible results he promised which would come from it. I saw it in my personal life through the countless trophies and recognitions I won through forensics and theater.

Mr. Hitt never had kids, and yet he treated me like his son. He saw my need, not only for physical resources such as food and money, but also my need for a mentor because of dad's death. He gave me everything he possibly could to make my life easier the rest of my high school years.

Mr. Hitt in person was a big guy, physically, but also larger than life. His accomplishments landed him in the Virginia High School League: Hall of Fame, and beyond this his contributions to humanity have been etched in the hearts of every good deed he has done for others, especially mine.

If Mr. Hitt called me today, and asked me to do something for him, my response would be:

"What do you need, Boss?"

Chapter 8

Angels Among Us

In one day, we as human beings will take over 21,000 breaths, and 6,201 steps. An estimate of seven billion people live on the Earth, so what does one person mean? Whether it was Martin Luther King Jr. whose voice boomed, "I Have a Dream" and challenged the roots of racism, or Mother Teresa whose hands and heart touched the lives of the sick and the dying in India; or whether it was the grim smile of Adolf Hitler, as the killing of innocent Jewish people began, or the last words of Jim Jones to his religious followers, shortly before leading them all to suicide, it can be seen that ONE person can change and affect the lives of millions of others. One person can change the world; whether it's for the good or bad.

Every individual is unique, each person has dreams goals and aspirations, but beyond our dreams and differences, are our similarities. Each person will take over 21,000 breaths, and 6,201 steps in a day. It's what we do with those breaths, those steps, those moments of life, that even though they seem dull to us at times, that step or breath, could be our last.

I had started to pick up steam as an activist, and public speaker in our local area, and started to receive many requests from organizations in the area to come and speak at churches, rallies, or governmental organization going into my senior year of high school.

That year I had been recognized and awarded the Boys and Girls Club of Central Virginia: Youth of the Year award for not only my work as an activist and motivational speaker but also because of my outreach and community service.

Over the course of my senior year of high school at Madison County High School, I saw a lot of things, experienced a lot of joy, and ultimately feel that I grew exponentially through it. If there was any other than 2011 that made an impact on my life, it was certainly my senior year at MCHS.

You know, I wasn't always a Madison kid. Honestly, when I moved to Madison county in fourth grade I wasn't too sure how things would go, nor did I have any idea if I would make friends. Typical thoughts of a 9 year old.

I came in on the first day and sat in my assigned seat. A quirky little fellow, the size of a twig, came in and sat next to me. His name was Lane Warren.

The first assignment we were given by our teacher Mrs. Moorehead, who Lane and I often doodled pictures of alligators eating her leg off, was a "get-to-know-you" assignment in which we had to draw and use color pencils to describe ourselves. The beginning of our friendship started when Lane looked over at me, broke out his colored pencils and started coloring outside the lines of everything he just drew. That day after he turned it into to our teacher I never got to see what was on it.

Years passed and through those years of elementary school to middle school Lane and I developed a friendship that was unique only to us; we'd hang out on the weekends and play video games, or hunker down in my room and play tons of Yu-Gi-Oh.

We'd shoot paintball at each other, or simply just talk about life. We talked about why we were here, where we were going, what we wanted to do, who we wanted to marry - we were kids. Eighth grade year he bugged me to come play on the soccer team, and sure enough I was kicking that damn ball in the grass with him.

When dad passed away, in the back, standing along the back wall because there were simply no seats left in the funeral home to sit there was Lane. Lane was my one of my best friends, despite growing apart from him during high school because of some choices he started making.

Sophomore year and junior year still stick vividly in my mind, as I remember him sleeping in nearly every class we had. He would wake up just long enough for him and I to play chess, like the inner nerd in us was used to.

Lane, on the night of homecoming 2013 in October, flipped his car several times, and was ejected from the drivers seat; injuring his date and taking his life. The silence of the hallways, the sight of classmates hugging each other, and the feeling of tears rolling down my own cheek, the day we returned to school after his tragic death, made me think back to the first time I met him.

Most of all, I thought about the "get-to-know-you" assignment that Lane was scribbling outside of the lines on. In our own lives, we've all hurt, we've all had those times when nothing has gone our way and we are forced to color outside the lines of everything we just tried to draw. And it's in times like those when we color outside the lines of our life that we think the world is over, that nothing good could come out of it. But it's times like those, and times like these that we need to step back and realize what it is we just did. I never got to see what Lane colored all those years ago, but I finally see it now when I saw so many people coming together to be strong for each other - the picture Lane colored so many years ago was the masterpiece of his life, and I step back and can see it in all its beauty.

It all happened so fast, and our student body didn't know how to respond. We just came together and mended each other's broken hearts. We clung to each other and made sure we were there, one for the other. We were all so confused, and even though I had dealt with death prior to Lane's, I still felt like I had a rug pulled out from underneath my feet.

The months following his death, I spent a lot of time just trying to figure out where to go from there. Many times, if you stay still long enough, life will continue to move around you. The only thing I am sure of in life is that everything changes, and if you do not adapt you will perish.

My freshman year, second semester, I took Mrs. Gail Temple's drama class. I'll never forget the day she assigned us textbook work, and in the quietness of taking notes I will never forget hearing a voice booming from the room next door, telling his students about Beowulf.

Mrs. Temple explained that it was Mr. McSherry. I'll always remember asking myself the question, "Who is Mr. McSherry, and why is he getting so excited about a poem written in the dark ages?" That day, I began my quest to find out more about Mr. McSherry. Walking into his room to meet him, any feelings of nervousness or fear were completely wiped away by that loving smile of his.

Time passed, and a genuine friendship developed. I will never be able to look past the numerous conversations about his travels to Thailand, politics, literature, music, or why wearing briefs instead of boxers is better for you as a man. Being in Mr. McSherry's presence made me realize the beauty of the simplest of things. He showed so much care for all of his students, even those who gave him trouble, in a way that I will never be able to describe it to those who didn't know him. He was so meek, mild, calm, and Christlike. After school, each day at forensics practice, he would give several students a hug, and then walk down the hallway and recycle all of the Dr. Pepper cans he had drank that day. His hugs would take away all the pain in your heart.

Before leaving for the National Speech and Debate Association's national tournament that summer, I ran upstairs to see him, and I gave him a huge hug. In that moment, I told him that I was going to work on making him proud at the tournament, and he responded saying, "Aw, Tristan. You can't do that. You've already made me so proud."

That was the summer before my senior year, and it was also the same summer that he diagnosed with pancreatic cancer. He had gone in because his back was hurting, but it turned out to be a lot more.

He fought, but in public it seemed he already had won. Nothing about his cancer seemed to phase him. He remained the same meek and humble Perry McSherry.

When has passed away, tears made my heart swell with grief, but the question I asked myself freshman year came back into my mind.

"Who is Mr. McSherry, and why is he getting so excited about a poem written in the dark ages?"

He loved his students. No matter what you did to that man, he would still give you the shirt off his back if you needed it. He brought so much enthusiasm to teaching, because of his love for us. He wanted us to grasp concepts of literature and also live by them, and so the only way he knew how to do that was bring stories or poems of the past to life.

So that is the answer to the last part of the question, but who is Mr. McSherry? In words his spirit could never be described, and his heart could never be contained in a series of sentences. His selflessness, compassion, and love for all who walked through his door, or by it, was immeasurable. He was greater than this life, and greater than the cancer that took him from this earth.

Losing him the students who were close to him were affected deeply, but this loss was felt deeply by the faculty who knew him. Within one year, we had lost two people that used to walk the high school daily.

We all continued to just hold to each other, and we remained so strong for no other reason than other being strong. You often don't know how strong you are until being strong is the only option you have. We didn't know how we were going to rebound from these losses, but all we were focused on was getting to the date of graduation.

I've been thinking about this day a lot lately.

When everything broke apart, we found a way to rise - together.

Months before we had all huddled into the gym to remember Lane at his memorial service, and months after that we practiced our graduation ceremonies without Mr. McSherry standing in the aisle with other teachers. And to think even with those two angels watching the ceremony in the rafters, we had an angel sitting in the first row, unknown to all of us that she would be joining them too.

What I would give to see that smile of Kaitlin Aylor one more time.

Kaitlin was one of the few girls in our high school that played more than one sport. Volleyball and softball, she was there - and then she quietly, and humbly would go home in he big ol' truck and probably hunt the next day if she had the time.

When she heard I was considering going to Eastern Mennonite, she became their biggest recruit. Everyday she'd come up to me and say, "Do the right thing. Go to school with me." Now I am sitting at VCU wishing I could turn back the hands of time to be with her again freshman year at MCHS.

Ping pong wasn't her strong suit. In fact, she was awful at it. I can remember her coming over to play, and taking out three extra balls just so she could get four points in one turn. How was I going to beat the master of goofiness? I did the only thing I could think of, and so I beat her using two paddles. Those moments of goofiness, those moments of pure happiness, they will probably never fade away, which will make the pain of losing her even greater.

From throwing apple wedges at her from a friend's truck or playing four square and dominating the competition at Boys and Girls club, talking about life, relationships, college, or where at in Mrs. Breckenridge's office I hid her purse, it's what made Kaitlin and I, what we were.

I'll never forget one of our last conversations.

It was about whether or not she should get a tattoo. She was so scared! After awhile though, she realized it is something you really wanted. She got a tattoo of an anchor. We talked a lot about the meaning of it all and why she wanted it. Her answer: Hebrews 6:19. Hope does the same thing for us as an anchor does for a ship. The meaning of the tattoo was that she believed so much in hope, and the anchor was her way to stay grounded in this crazy life.

Everything you did Kaitlin, was so small and that's what impressed me the most about her. How she could do the littlest thing and it would make me smile like a fool.

In life, there is so much that comes against us as human beings. We can have a multitude of problems in our relationships, finances, careers, etc. and those problems cause us to live in fear of what we could be if we only believe in our talents.

This is the part where I am suppose to tell everybody, not to give up hope, to smile brighter than the darkness around them, but all of that at a time like this, just seems shallow. As a man who believes in God, the words "I'll pray for you", even seem shallow to me. Almost as if they hold no meaning anymore, but in the midst of chaos we have to trust that somewhere, among it all, God is there.

Some how, through the tears, and the frustration, we have to appreciate what life is: a gift. And whether you are religious or not, even though the pain hurts, and the anger is raging, we all have a responsibility to lean on each other. Each of us, are just one person. We have burdens, and baggage that we carry day to day, but together, we are strong. Yes, it only takes one person to change the world, but imagine, just imagine, what hundreds and thousands of us could do if we began loving deeper than we ever have, or began showing compassion to people we would never, even in our wildest of dreams, speak to.

My heart is breaking just writing this, reliving some of the tragic events that happened in the past year. The idea that some of the most important people in life can be gone in an instant answers the question I asked at the beginning of the chapter.

What does one person mean?

My answer?

Everything.

Chapter 9

The Professor and His Baseball Cap

It all started with dad's blonde hair, blue eyes, and a dream in his heart. He was determined to make an impact on the world, and to do so in a way where his world would be change forever as well. Clothes that were stuffed in suitcases were then stuffed in the back of the family car. From there, the journey began. Stepping out, eyes looking to the sky, filled with skyscrapers and opportunity, he had found his home.

In our American culture you are promised twelve years of education. Twelve long years of struggling through multiplication tables, chapter books, and excessive amount of homework. Beyond the workload of school, but still a part of the American public education system, was the drama, the drama, the drama and of course, that weird mystery meat the cafeteria served every Wednesday. In our American society, this high school experience is one of growth, and the memories and knowledge imparted shouldn't stop, but continue to grow.

To pursue higher education in our society in our society, is to secure a clearer future. As shown in a unemployment report for the month of September, 2013, people without a college degree of any kind were more likely to be unemployed, while those with a degree had found work or were more likely to be hired. Through securing a college degree, you secure for yourself more opportunities of educational growth, and therefore, broaden your scope of knowledge. Simply attending a community college, or a vocational/trade school, advances your understanding of the world we live in, and better qualifies you to give input on the topic or area of study that you examined outside of high school. Because many high schools do not offer the ability to magnify an area their students personally wish to study, higher education allows a student to pursue that which their heart desires, and ultimately, allows for them to enter the workforce well versed in their profession.

Attending a university or college of higher education is solely about learning. However, one should understand that learning does not simply take place by reading a textbook, but through discussions and interactions with classmates, who may or may not share the same viewpoint as the method being introduced. Higher education provides you with the ability to develop sincere relationships with classmates and peers, while providing you with a safe academic environment for you to learn from one another. Colleges and universities provide you the elements for growth; not only textbooks and harder assignments, but people. The people you will meet through higher education, good and bad, will yield more unforgettable memories and also valuable life experience. To be in communication with other beings is where true education and learning begins. Through thorough studies of textbooks and listening to the lectures of experienced professors, we grow in professional knowledge. Through the interactions with those around campus we expound upon the knowledge found in books, and begin to see education come to life. Growth in these relationships, and new beginnings with others are often overlooked reasons for attending college, but for myself it is the number one reason.

In 1988, after graduating high school, he left home. It all started with blonde hair, blue eyes, and a dream in his heart. He was determined to make an impact on the world, and to do so in a way where his world would be change forever as well. Clothes that were stuffed in suitcases were then stuffed in the back of the family car. From there, the journey began. Stepping out, eyes looking to the sky, filled with skyscrapers and opportunity, he had found his home.

Virginia Commonwealth University and the city lights of Richmond gave him a sense of hope, a sense of belonging. There he met friends who went on to become actors, artists, and teachers. Within that span, he met his future wife, and the bearer of his only child. Four years later, 1992, he returned home, with a bachelors degree in art history. His life had only begun before attending college, and now, after, it began to flourish. My father's dream of attending college, over twenty five years ago, is now my own. Like him I packed my bags and embarked on my own journey, and I have not looked back at all.

Out of high school, I decided to attend Virginia Commonwealth in the fall of 2014. It was a tough decision, choosing VCU over 5 other schools that offered me so much. Choosing VCU allowed me to breathe in a sense of opportunity and with that breathe out natural success.

The city of Richmond was so opposite of the little small town that I had known. Richmond was known for it's community of artists, lawmakers, and skyscrapers, while Madison was known for having more cows than people. In contrast, VCU and the city of Richmond, provided me with the ability to grow in an area and environment that I was unfamiliar with, alongside people who were doing the same.

In life, you either adapt or perish. That's evolution. People in Richmond moved faster than I did. They were acclimated to the idea that you had to go after the things you want now rather than later, because there is someone else with the same skillset who desires the same thing you do. Dreams belong to those who desire to make them come true. Ambition, hard work, dedication, and resiliency are among the many traits I learned from millionaires, politicians, coaches and teachers since being at VCU.

However, the most influencing trait learned was self-forgiveness.

My first semester, I took Psychology 101: Introduction to Psychology. My professor was a man by the name of Dr. Everett Worthington. Dr. Worthington is a short man, with a white beard and glasses that sat upon his nose just right. His smile charmed all of us in the 300+ student class, and his jokes made us smile right back, mainly because they were so cheesy. Every single class, he'd come in to class and swiftly walk to the front of the room, removing his baseball cap that he always wore.

At first glance, Dr. Worthington seems like someone you would be great friends with. However, Dr. Worthington challenged us all in ways I could never be able to explain to anyone who has never understood his personal background.

Everett Worthington was born in 1946, in Knoxville, Tennessee. In 1968, he received a bachelors degree from the University of Tennessee in nuclear engineering and later went to Massachusetts Institute of Technology in 1970 receiving his MSNE. From there, he served as an active duty naval officer from 1970 to 1974, teaching nuclear physics at the Naval Nuclear Power School. He resigned his commission in 1979, having achieved the rank of Lieutenant.

Dr. Worthington often joked in class about how boring his life was but from the paragraph above his life was anything but boring. Worthington however describes it as boring because he desired a different journey for himself. He graduated from the University of Missouri with a masters in Psychology in 1976, and then two years later, 1978, received his doctorate degree.

Dr. Worthington began his work at Virginia Commonwealth University in the summer of 1989. Dr. Worthington's work is far greater than how human behavior is affected by the human mind.

Rather, the bulk of his work is found in something more far reaching than the inner workings of the human mind. As things in his personal life built up walls of chaos and torment around him, Dr. Worthington examined the human soul and what could be done to alleviate the agony it felt.

One thing you learn very quickly of the professor with the baseball cap, is that he is not reserved for a specific reason other than he knows that if you reveal everything in one class, you don't have anything left to further share. So, Dr. Worthington would work with us, all 300+, by sharing elements of his personal life, humor, and love each class, while each time we'd walk out feeling more and more refreshed than when we arrived, or the class before. Dr. Worthington had been practicing psychology and counseling longer than he had been teaching it in a college setting and beyond his vocational practice of counseling and psychology he applied it personally.

In 1996, while he was away on vacation, Dr. Worthington's mother's home in Knoxville was broken into on New Years day and in the startle of her home being broken into, she was awoken and murdered by the burglar. She was 76 years old.

Dr. Worthington's brother was the person who found his mother lying on the floor. Because of this, his brother went through great pain, feeling as if it was his fault. Dr. Worthington told us how on Saturday's his brother would just go into his room, and draw the blinds to sit in darkness.

In 2005, nine years after their mother's murder, Dr. Worthington's brother committed suicide. This is what truly broke Dr. Worthington in ways he could not describe. He felt so much self-condemnation for his brother's suicide, like he should've done more as a licensed psychologist to help him. Dr. Worthington struggled with that demon every day.

Dr. Worthington became so vulnerable with us, and told us about how this self-condemnation ate at him, but one day that all changed. Walking along Jupiter beach. Dr. Worthington found comfort in an image he created created using natural surroundings. He was walking that morning on the beach and stubbed his toe on a piece of coral. He took mounds of sand and piled it on top of the piece of coral and then atop the sand he placed seashells he had found.

Dr. Worthington felt his heart was like the coral, buried by a mound of sand or self-condemnation and guilt, which separated him from the shells or his idea of God's love. This separation was only what was apparent to him, but not the truth, because when the waves washed of the ocean came in and washed away the sand, it left only the shells touching the coral. This realization showed Dr. Worthington that nothing can separate us from the love of God. (Romans 8:35)

Dr. Worthington helped me realize that we are "flawed but precious" in God's eyes. No matter the mistakes we've made, no matter we feel we deserve as punishment because of what we've done, no matter what others have done or said about us to make us feel less than, God does not see that nor does He allow it to separate His love for us. God sees us as His creation and His joy; regardless of what we've done.

Dr. Worthington's life is a testament to this. Had he continued to believe that his self-condemnation, and judgement of himself separated him from the inseparable love God has for his children than I do not think I would've been sitting in a psychology class at VCU taught by Dr. Worthington but rather someone else.

Self-forgiveness was the doorway for Dr. Worthington to reexamine everything self-condemning thing he thought and said about himself, however, it was not the destination. The destination for Dr. Worthington was to be able to teach this knowledge to countless young people at the fulcrum of their lives.

Dr. Worthington's writings and teachings are the foundation for which we can all live harmoniously lives as we did before major trauma. His is a lifetime of work and pain that will stand the test of time, because of the principles it contains inside but also because the words he has written were from the tears of the soul, and shows us the reflection of ourselves.

VCU was the intersection of my life and Dr. Worthington's. His work transformed my life, and my outlook on who I am to myself, to others and to God. For during that same first semester of college in which I met Dr. Worthington, I was dealing with a loss that I thought I was personally responsible for. A loss that I felt if I had given more of myself and resources to that I would not have lost that individual from my life.

God never brings someone into your life without purpose.

Dr. Worthington told my class at the end of the semester that he was no longer going to teach, but that he was going to spend the rest of his time at VCU researching. To look back as these words are being written, read them, and see how far I've come because of what I learned from Dr. Worthington's personal example, I am humbled that I was able to sit in the last class he ever taught at VCU.

We are flawed, but precious.

Chapter 10

....

The Water Hose

If you made it this far, you've seen that this book is designed to be more than just an autobiography. I started writing this in 2011, and what started out as journals to help ease the pain of dad's death, started taking shape in the form of a literary work. I wrote this book to be not so much to tell about myself, but rather an attempt for me to share personal anecdotes with you in order to help you learn from my mistakes, my pain, my success, so that you can reach greater heights!

I'm sure you've been wondering why this book is called "The Water Hose", and this is the final chapter, the one that will solidify everything, pull everything together, or maybe it will do the opposite.

Maybe, it will confuse you, leave you wondering for more, and cause you to step out to live a life that is daring and adventurous to find the meaning of what this book was all about.

If you remember nothing from this book, I want you to remember this one thing:

My father loved Tina Ragen.

With all his heart, mind, and soul, Randy James wanted to give Tina Ragen the world.

Before dad asked Tina to marry him, he wanted to prove his worth to her and show her how much she meant to him. One thing he missed from his upbringing was gardening. Dad had the vision of building Tina a garden in the back yard, as well as growing grass where there was none.

One day he spent the whole day at Lowes looking at buying long pieces of wood to create raised flower beds, flowers to grow, seed to bring new life with and much more. He wanted this to be perfect. In his mind, if he accomplished this he would feel as if he had done something for her which made her truly happy.

Once he had his materials, he went back to the house and started building. He laid the boards of wood across the piles of mulch that he had placed in the hole he dug. He placed the flowers in the new bed he had made, patted each down, and then went back in the house satisfied with the work he had done.

Tina came home and was so surprised and so thankful for dad's hard work. Dad loved her, and to him the sweat and labor was easy in return for all the support she had given him.

After building the garden it's upkeep was the next thing.

The day my dad told me it was my responsibility to water the plants was the day I wanted to run as fast as I could. I hated the idea of having to water the plants. I thought it was boring and I didn't want my best friend, Alex Minor, who lived next door to see me watering the plants and make fun of me later.

One of the hardest parts of watering the plants was rolling the water hose back up. To me this was the hardest thing about watering the plants, and to me probably the most stressful job on the planet. Having to put back the water hose from it's jumbled mess is something I always had problems with.

Dad went inside and left me to water the plants. An hour later, he came back out and saw me there more or less in a pretzel, tangled up in the water hose trying to get it back on the wheel.

"What are you doing, boy?", he shouted.

As if he couldn't see how I had basically tied my hands and feet up, had the hose in a ball, and was no where close to getting the hose back into the wheel. I had already watered the plants. That was not the problem. The problem was simply that damn water hose.

All he could do is simply laugh and look at me with nothing but a smile on his face. He walked down the stairs of the deck and then started to make joke after joke about how funny it was to see me in the predicament I was in. Meanwhile, I wanted him to hurry up and get down the stairs to free me from the hell I was in.

In that moment, my dad issued me the most important piece of fatherly wisdom he ever had.

"Son, it's just a water hose. Don't let it kick your ass."

I was entangled by a piece of vinyl. That shouldn't happen to people. It shouldn't take as long as it did to put the hose back. Instead, that water hose took me hours to put back on the wheel, and all my dad could say was:

"Don't let it kick your ass."

It was this sentence that has become my mantra in my life.

Life is like a water hose. At times it becomes so confusing. Things happen and don't make sense when it happens. The hardest part about life is that it is a little bit more complex than a water hose, however, through my I've not found a greater metaphor to help me understand life.

So many moments of our lives are caught up and defined by moments of extreme chaos. The chaos leads to our tangling. Before you know it our lives like a water hose are transformed into a giant ball of vinyl. The pain of being fired from your job has led to difficulties in your marriage. Injuring yourself on the field and the ending of your sports career led to depression. The abuse you suffered from as a child led to the feelings of unworthiness you have today.

Like the water hose when you get one kink, there usually is a kink somewhere else. Every kink in the hose inhibits the flow of water. The flow of water is so desperately needed for filling basins, or the growth of seeds. Nothing grows without water and the sun.

Life is like the water hose.

Our kinks inhibit the flow of our talents. Our talents are the agent which gives life to our dreams, and causes them to grow. When this thing or that thing happens to us over the course of our lives, it's hard to get back up and keep fighting, and this in turn causes us to become discouraged and prevents us from giving our all to becoming the next pro-football player, the next business owner, the next author.

The problems of life are so incredibly hard to overcome.

However, it is not impossible to overcome the pain of the past!

What is possible is to live a life of victory, health and success. The situations you've been dealt are what you've been given not to be derailed by, but rather you've been given these challenges to learn from and to drive you even more than you've ever been before.

Whatever happened to you thirty years ago, ten years ago, five years ago, yesterday, is not the end of your story. Your life shouldn't be based on what others believe about you or on what has happened to you. Your life should be based around what you are going to do, and always around the dream you are trying to grow.

In life, all you have to do is supply the water, those uncanny talents of yours that no one else has. The sun, the warmth of God's love, will take care of the rest. God's love for you is like the sun. You don't have to understand anything about God to feel the warmth of His love.

I've learned that over the years as I've experienced heartache and failure that through it all, no matter what, God was there. I've learned that God is with you wherever you go, and through whatever decision you make. That's it. If you make a decision to join the military, God is there. If you decide to start your own business, God is there. If you do something else or join the circus - God is there with you.

Sometimes though, because of situations we experience as people the dreams we have become overshadowed by fear and we forget to water them, so they stop growing. We think that what we have to offer to the world is inadequate or that our talents are not as valuable as those of someone else, and so we decide that rather than giving life to our dreams, it is best to sit back and see what happens.

We rely too heavily on luck and chance. We'd rather wait for the rain to water our dreams then be proactive and do it for ourselves. We have become a society that has become so satisfied by complacency and filled with so much doubt that we are pleased to see very little growth in our dreams over time. We have become a society where working long hours and more than one job is the norm, and doing things that we ultimately do not like is average.

Why are you allowing your happiness to be delayed?

You can be happy **now**!

But to achieve the outcome you desire nothing can happen without a decision.

You have two choices. Live the life you've always dreamed of by giving life to your dreams every day or sit back and hope for the best. If you choose the first one, it will require a lot of work to succeed. You will have to get up everyday, look yourself in the mirror and tell yourself how great you are. If you choose the second option, you will not have to do anything, and have to live with the death of your dreams. Nothing grows without water, and while the sun will shine on your dream, it takes your talent and effort to be the ultimate agent that changes a seed into a beautiful flower.

I hope you find a clear answer so that you feel confident about this decision, but you might not. Even if you make a choice and still feel anxious about that choice, unsure what the future holds - well, God is right there with you in the midst of all that, too.

You don't have to do anything other than remove the kinks that are keeping you from releasing the talents that cause the growth. I promise you, even when it seems like the world is against you, if you keep walking despite it all, you will find that it is turning for you, and spinning in your favor.

The Bible says in the eighth chapter of Psalms that the Earth is filled with the glory of God, and even though Earth is just a tiny dot in the corner of the universe everything on it is filled with his glory.

It's so hard not to see beauty in a sunrise, strength in the trees, hope in the stars, ourselves in other people. I know it's hard to see the clearing when it seems like there are so many obstacles in our path. The hardest thing about it all is that we can't control most of what happens to us, but we can choose how we will respond to it and how we will answer to the pain we've found ourselves in.

The best you is emerging, and the real you is showing up. You are the head and not the tail. You are the blessed, not the cursed. You are the rich, not the poor. You are the healed, not the sick. You are the lender, not the borrower. You are a dreamer!

Become the victor of your adversity! Don't give up on your dreams!

Life will bring tests and pain. However, you've been created to be happy, fearless, loved. So in those times when it feels like giving up is your only option, don't.

I went to Los Angeles during the summer of 2014.

When I got off the plane, the palm trees that greeted me, the cool breeze, the beauty of the mountains, all of it was simply breathtaking. I loved Los Angeles, as it was the city of dreamers.

I think what impressed me the most wasn't the skyscrapers or the malls, the millions of things to do or the opportunities. The thing that impressed me the most was simply a father and son.

I stayed in Los Angeles with my dad's college roommate, Travis Stanberry. Going out west was a personal journey for me because Travis truly is one of the last extensions of my dad that I have. Travis told hilarious stories about my dad in college. He told me how they drove all night to North Carolina to play video games with one of their friends who had dropped out of college and then all the way back to Virginia the next day.

Seeing Travis interact with his son made me realize and replay all the moments I had with my dad. Travis reminded me of how ambitious dad was, and how thoughtful he was of others. Not hearing my dad's voice in three years has made the memories fade and the pain grow, but Travis reminded me of how beautiful that man truly is. Meeting 7 year old Jackson, Travis' son, was also life changing for me, because it ensures that the bond made back all those years ago during their time together at VCU between Travis and my father will continue through the second generation and generations after that.

I don't know where my dad is, but I know he's smiling down on the life I am living because the life I am living is all for him. And surprisingly, when I take it all in - having incredible people by my side, the success, the opportunities - I know he's close by.

After I was named "Youth of the Year" by the Boys and Girls Club of Central Virginia, I was asked to give a speech at their annual Kentucky Derby fundraiser. I went with the intentions of just simply telling my story, and that's what I did. I talked about life, dad, and what the Boys and Girls Club meant to me.

The beauty of that night wasn't found in the elaborate hats, or the lavish food that was seen/eaten, but in the eyes of an elderly lady from the community, who after I spoke came to me and told me about losing her husband and how my speech inspired her. This is the true meaning of life, to care for one another in their time of grief and brokenness. I'll never be able to forget the tears she left on my suit jacket as she asked me for a hug. These are the moments I live for.

For me money or fame isn't the impetus of my life.

I want to help.

I want to inspire.

To love, and be loved.

That should be our goal as human beings. Because no matter what happens in this world, or what we gain for ourselves materially, there will always be other people who need us. There will always be other people that at the end of the day need a hand to be extended to them so that they can keep fighting.

When a flower grows it drops seeds into other places and causes the growth of other plants. When you start to see your dreams grow, I challenge you to do what you can to sow into the dreams of others. Drop your seeds of greatness into other places of the ground.

When you do so, you will feel fulfilled.

Whatever you are going through, fight!

And if you see others who are getting weary, lift them up.

The beauty of the water hose, the beauty of life, is that, even in it's tangled confusion, it still has a beginning and an end. Similarly, in life, things may not make sense in the moment, and we are actively trying to get it 'untangled', but have hope, because the pain you are going through now, which doesn't make any sense, will eventually find itself wrapped back together like a water hose, and you'll find your heart beating louder again!

"It's just a water hose. Don't let it kick your ass."

About the Author

Tristan is a former Youth of the Year at the Boys and Girls Club of Central Virginia, former three-time Virginia high-school league state champion in forensics and debate, and the recipient of many other awards and acknowledgements for his humanitarian work. Currently, Tristan resides in Richmond, Virginia, where he is a student at Virginia Commonwealth University.

Printed in the United States
By Bookmasters